HEAVENLY HASH

Inspirational
Wit, Wisdom, and Whimsy

Barbour Books, Westwood, New Jersey

Scripture taken from the HOLY BIBLE, NEW INTERNATIONAL VERSION. Copyright © 1973, 1978, 1984 by International Bible Society.

Published by **Barbour and Company, Inc., P.O. Box 1219, Westwood, New Jersey 07675.**

Typesetting by Typetronix, Inc., Cape Coral, Florida

ISBN 1-55748-252-7

Printed in the United States of America

1 2 3 4 5 / 96 95 94 93 92 91

If instead of a gem, or even a flower, we could cast the gift of a lovely thought into the heart of a friend, that would be giving as the angels give.

GEORGE MacDONALD

We don't have to try to be something we're not with God. He knows us better than we know ourselves.

The betrayal of Jesus by Judas Iscariot was initiated by Judas, not by the chief priests. *(Matthew 26:14)*

Nazareth to Bethlehem is approximately seventy miles as the crow flies. As the donkey trots, it's about a three-day trip.

If we understand God, then we must believe in His miracles.

I praise you because I am fearfully
and wonderfully made; your works
are wonderful, I know that full well.

Psalm 139:14 (NIV)

Abraham had two nephews named Uz and Buz. *(Genesis 22:21)*

When Abraham told people that Sarah was his sister, he was only half lying. They had the same father.

(Genesis 20:12)

Keep your face to the sunshine
and you cannot see the shadow.

—*Helen Keller*

For he chose us in him before the creation of the world to be holy and blameless in his sight.

Ephesians 1:4 (NIV)

While in a Philippian jail, Paul and Silas prayed and sang hymns at midnight. *(Acts 16:25)*

"Apple of your eye" is hardly a new expression. Solomon said it in Proverbs 7:2.

Never take anything for granted.
—*Benjamin Disraeli*

Teach us to number our days aright,
that we may gain a heart of wisdom.
Psalm 90:12 (NIV)

Jonathan once killed a huge man who had six fingers on each hand and six toes on each foot.

(2 Samuel 21:20-21)

If you don't confine your ox that is known for killing people, and your ox kills somebody, you and your ox have to die. *(Exodus 21:29)*

One single grateful thought raised
to heaven is the most perfect prayer.

—*G. E. Lessing*

...Believe in the Lord Jesus, and you will be saved — you and your household. *Acts 16:31* (NIV)

If Samson loved his wife enough to kill for her, why did he call her a cow? *(Read Judges 14:18)*

The next time you see a picture of Noah's family looking young and agile, look twice. Noah's son Shem was ninety-eight when the flood came.

(Genesis 11:10)

The childhood shows the man,
As morning shows the day.

—John Milton

Above all, love each other deeply, because love covers over a multitude of sins.   *1 Peter 4:8* (NIV)

If you knock out your slave's tooth,
you have to set him free.

(Exodus 21:27)

As a result of Paul's imprisonment, early Christians became more fearless in speaking God's Word.

(Philippians 1:14)

God asks no man whether he will accept life. That is not the choice. You must take it. The only choice is how.   —*Henry Ward Beecher*

...I am ready not only to be bound, but also to die in Jerusalem for the name of the Lord Jesus.

Acts 21:13 (NIV)

Never afraid to be a witness, Paul was labeled a "babbler" by Athenian philosophers.   *(Acts 17:16-18)*

While Deborah judged Israel, the people lived in peace for forty years. Behind every peaceful country, there is a good woman. *(Judges 5:31)*

Too many people think that being a Christian means believing but not doing.

And if Christ has not been raised, our preaching is useless and so is your faith.   *1 Corinthians 15:14* (NIV)

Pharoah's daughter named the baby she found Moses because she "drew him out of the water."   *(Exodus 2:10)*

Those soldiers in Israel's army who were "fainthearted" were allowed to go home, lest they cause others to feel likewise.   *(Deuteronomy 20:8)*

When we get thrown into the lions' den, it feels like the only way we can hope to avoid being eaten is to become a lion ourselves.

Blessed is he who has regard for the weak; the Lord delivers him in times of trouble.   *Psalm 41:1* (NIV)

As Stephen was being stoned to death, he saw Jesus standing at the right hand of God. *(Acts 7:55)*

Both King Saul and the apostle Paul (Saul) trace their lineage to the tribe of Benjamin.   *(Acts 13:21)*

The distance is nothing; it is only the first step that is difficult.

—*Mme du Deffand*

Do two walk together unless they have agreed to do so? *Amos 3:3* (NIV)

The disciples were first called Christians in Antioch.   *(Acts 11:26)*

When God needed to punish David, he gave him three choices: three years of famine, three months of enemy pursuit, or three days of plague. Which would you choose?

(2 Samuel 24:13)

43

A good guideline to follow concerning the possessions of this world is to contemplate the question of what Christ might do with the same possessions if they were His.

Charm is deceptive, and beauty is fleeting; but a woman who fears the Lord is to be praised.

Proverbs 31:30 (NIV)

Peter paid taxes for Jesus and himself with money he found in a fish's mouth. Not so trivial, but pretty strange.

(Matthew 17:27)

When Paul was building a fire, a poisonous snake bit him on the hand. People thought he was a god when he didn't die. *(Acts 28:1–6)*

When you have nothing to say, say
nothing.   —*Charles Caleb Colton*

The grass withers and the flowers fall, but the word of our God stands forever. *Isaiah 40:8* (NIV)

A beautiful, indiscreet woman is like a gold ring in a pig's snout.

(Proverbs 11:22)

Don't eat things with wings.
(Leviticus 11:23)

Truth is the cry of all, but the game
of the few. —*Bishop Berkeley*

If a man dies, will he live again?
Job 14:14 (NIV)

For some reason, it took forty days to embalm a person back when Jacob was alive, or actually when Jacob was dead. *(Genesis 50:3)*

Isaiah went around stripped and bare-foot for three years as a sign against Egypt. *(Isaiah 20:3)*

How happy he who crowns in shades like these,

A youth of labour with an age of ease. —*Oliver Goldsmith*

How beautiful on the mountains are the feet of those who bring good news ....

Isaiah 52:7 (NIV)

Before a girl could be presented to King Xerxes, she had to put up with twelve months of beauty treatments.

(Esther 2:12)

The next time you wear a shawl,
you will be wearing a wimple.

(Ruth 3:15)

But far more numerous was the
herd of such
Who think too little and who talk too
much.   —*John Dryden*

I know that my Redeemer lives, and
that in the end He will stand upon
the earth.   *Job 19:25* (NIV)

Jesus fed the five thousand with five loaves and two fish. *(John 6:9)*

The wise men saw the star at least two times during their lengthy journey.

(Matthew 2:2,9)

No man is an island, entire of it-self; every man is a piece of the continent, a part of the main.

—*John Donne*

His eyes are on the ways of men;
he sees their every step. There is no
dark place, no deep shadow, where
evildoers can hide.

Job 34:21–22 (NIV)

David attempted to wear Saul's armor when he faced off with Goliath. At the time Saul had no idea that David had been anointed king.

(1 Samuel 16:13, 17:38)

Israel will become one nation, prophesied Ezekiel, and it will never again be divided into more than one kingdom. Prophecy fulfilled! *(Ezekiel 37:22)*

All men think all men mortal, but themselves.　　　*—Edward Young*

Set a guard, over my mouth, O Lord; keep watch over the door of my lips. *Psalm 141:3* (NIV)

Although John won the race with Peter to Jesus' tomb, Peter was the first to enter while John looked through the doorway. *(John 20:2–4, 6)*

Joshua and his army marched around Jericho seven times on the seventh day with seven priests blowing seven trumpets. *Joshua 6:3–4*

God has two dwellings: one in Heaven, and the other in a meek and thankful heart.

—*Izaak Walton*

He has made everything beautiful
in its time. He has also set eternity
in the hearts of men.

Ecclesiastes 3:11 (NIV)

Elijah felt the presence of the Lord
in a "still, small voice."

(1 Kings 19:11-13)

Jesus told His disciples three times that He would be put to death and would rise from the dead.

(Matthew 16:21; 17:22-23; 20:17-19)

Ah, but a man's reach should exceed
　　his grasp,
Or what's a heaven for?

　　　　　　　　　　　—*Robert Browning*

John said that if all that Jesus had done were recorded, "the whole world would not have room for the books that would be written."

John 21:25 (NIV)

Lazarus had been in the tomb four days when Jesus arrived.

(John 11:17)

Israelites weren't allowed to eat camels. What a sacrifice! Well, actually, they couldn't sacrifice them either.

(Leviticus 11:4)

Think of it! God is actually waiting to hear from us.

Pray also for me, that whenever I open my mouth, words may be given me so that I will fearlessly make known the mystery of the gospel.

Ephesians 6:19 (NIV)

Paul performed unusual miracles in Ephesus using handkerchiefs and aprons to heal diseases. A true man of the cloth! *(Acts 19:11-12)*

Goodbye, face lifts. As a sign to Hezekiah that he would have a longer life, God caused the shadow on the sundial to go back ten degrees.

(2 Kings 20:8–11)

For each age is a dream that is
dying,
Or one that is coming to birth.

—Arthur O'Shaughnessy

Like a city whose walls are broken
down is a man who lacks self-control.

Proverbs 25:28 (NIV)

The Israelites were forbidden to eat pork because pigs do not chew the cud. *(Deuteronomy 14:8)*

The Israelites crossed the Red Sea on dry ground, of course. But this miracle was repeated a few more times on occasions that evidently don't rate a Hollywood effort.

God help the Minister that meddles
with art.   —*Lord Melbourne*

What has been will be again, what
has been done will be done again;
There is nothing new under the sun.

Ecclesiastes 1:9 (NIV)

The only requirement for the Israelites who wished to donate materials to build the tabernacle was that they have a willing heart.

(Exodus 35:5, 22, 29)

During Solomon's reign, there was so much wealth in Jerusalem that silver was as plenteous as stones.

(1 Kings 10:27)

Noise provides us with a place to hide, where we don't have to face ourselves. Be still, and know that God is there.

... We are the clay, you our potter;
we are all the work of your hand.

Isaiah 64:8 (NIV)

Here's a phrase that has stood the test of time—Job was the first recorded person to say "the skin of my teeth."   *(Job 19:20)*

To your health? Moses burned the golden calf, ground it to powder, poured it on the water, and made the Israelites drink it.   *(Exodus 32:20)*

When we don't receive credit and acclaim, we feel cheated. What we need to remember is that none of our actions goes unnoticed by God.

The fear of the Lord is the beginning of wisdom, and knowledge of the Holy One is understanding.

Proverbs 9:10 (NIV)

When Isaac carried the wood to Mt. Moriah for Abraham, he did not know that he was to be the sacrifice.

(Genesis 22:7)

Locusts, katydids, crickets, and grasshoppers were considered clean food for the Israelites. What's for lunch?

(Leviticus 11:22)

Share your faith. Ask someone to church with you. You never know what might happen.

Before a word is on my tongue you
know it completely, O Lord.

Psalm 139:4 (NIV)

Two women who knew how to dress
for success: Esther succeeded Vashti
as queen of Persia.   *(Esther 2:17)*

None of the Israelites' children who was born during the forty years in the wilderness was circumcised.

(Joshua 5:5)

It is by the goodness of God that in our country we have those three unspeakably precious things: freedom of speech, freedom of conscience, and the prudence never to practice either of them. —*Mark Twain*

Hannah made a promise to God that if He gave her a son he would belong to the Lord and no razor would come upon his head. A promise with strands attached!

(1 Samuel 1:11)

God gave us the Bible as a comfort and a support, not as a topic for debate.

Pilate reported three times that he could find no fault with Jesus.

(John 18:38; 19:4, 6)

Reflect upon your present blessings, of which every man has many; not upon your past misfortunes, of which all men have some.

—*Charles Dickens*

You are the salt of the earth. But if the salt loses its saltiness, how can it be made salty again?

Matthew 5:13 (NIV)

Ezekiel divided his hair into thirds
to depict three different ways Israel
would be destroyed in the Babylonian
conquest.   *(Ezekiel 5:1–2)*

When Lazarus came out of the grave, only his hands, feet, and face were wrapped with cloth.   *(John 11:44)*

The wages of sin is death, and yet it seems that we pursue sin believing that its wages are the finest reward we could possibly attain.

When praying or prophesying, a woman was to have her head covered. *(1 Corinthians 11:5)*

The only true power in this world is the power of God, and our fate will not be decided by men and women, but by God.

When Nineveh repented, its residents even put sackcloth on all their animals. *(Jonah 3:8)*

No one has the option to call himself a Christian and keep it selfishly inside.

What is the last verse of Psalms?
"Let everything that has breath praise
the Lord. Praise the Lord!"

Psalm 150:6 (NIV)

An idea whose time has come: Under Mosaic Law, if a man lent money to a poor fellow, he was not allowed to charge interest.

(Exodus 22:5)

The children of Israel ate manna for forty years. Wonder if they ever ate it again? *(Exodus 16:35)*

The better we understand the awe-some magnificence of God, the more we expose our own imperfection.

During the whole time the Israelites wandered around the desert,
they never got swollen feet.

(Deuteronomy 8:4)

The peace of the Lord is the strongest force on earth, and those who find peace in the Lord need never fear.

Once Jesus called demons out of a man and sent them into a herd of about 2000 pigs. *(Mark 5:13)*

Even God cannot change the past.
—*Agathon*

So, whether you eat or drink or whatever you do, do it all for the glory of God. *1 Corinthians 10:31* (NIV)

Once Ezekiel was sitting in his house when a big hand picked him up by the hair of his head and took him somewhere between heaven and earth. *(Ezekiel 8:3)*

Jonah was the only prophet to whom Jesus likened Himself: Jesus said He would be in the earth three days, the same length of time Jonah had been in the fish. *(Matthew 12:39–40)*

Fear of the Lord should not drive us from Him, but should help us to understand Him.

Flood waters remained on the earth for 150 days.   *(Genesis 7:24)*

The faith of a child is every bit as mighty as the faith of an older man or woman.

Christians will have a role in judging angels.   *(1 Corinthians 6:3)*

Earth has no sorrow that Heaven cannot heal.   —*Thomas Moore*

Israelites were forbidden to wear clothes made of two kinds of material. So much for 50% cotton/50% polyester.

(Leviticus 19:19)

Teach me to live, that I may dread
The grave as little as my bed.
—*Bishop Thomas Ken*

David wrote seventy-three of the one hundred fifty psalms in the book of Psalms.

Usually, we are on our best behavior when we know that someone else is around. The funny thing is, Somebody is ...

Solomon had 700 wives and 300 concubines. Anniversaries must have been a problem.

God blesses the person who realizes he or she is no better than anyone else.

Lots were cast by families to choose gate keepers in Jerusalem. No wonder. Who would volunteer for the Dung gate, anyway?

(1 Chronicles 26:3)

Jesus said that with the faith the size of a mustard seed, we could move mountains. How much could we accomplish if we had the commitment of a small ant?

It didn't rain in the Garden of Eden, or out of it for that matter. Water came up from the ground to make things grow. *(Genesis 2:5-6)*

And when we think we lead, we are most led.   *—Lord Byron*

The punishment for adultery was death for both parties. Instead of "I do," the vow might be "I won't!"

(Leviticus 20:10–12)

'Tis an awkward thing to play with
      souls,
And matter enough to save one's
own.   —*Robert Browning*

Meshech, the grandson of Shem, was also known as Mash (Hebrew). Wouldn't you use a different name too? *(1 Chronicles 1:17)*

Man is an embodied paradox, a bundle of contradictions.

—*Charles Caleb Colton*

We are individual, yet we bear the stamp of our Maker. God's image dwells within us all.

Be wisely worldly, be not worldly
wise.   —*Francis Quarles*

People weren't given permission to
eat meat until after the Flood.

(Genesis 9:3)

Judgment will come from the Lord. What should come from us is open and honest love, and the gift of a second chance.

God rejoices when we repay good
for good and love with love.

It is when we grow complacent that we stand in the greatest danger of losing that which is most important.

Like that of leaves is a generation
of men.   —*Homer*

The greatest legacy we can leave is a life well lived.

What do we live for if it is not to make life less difficult for each other?
—*George Eliot*

Often, wisdom comes without great fanfare. It comes to those who wait with open heart and mind.

What doesn't happen in a year can happen in a day.   —*Violet M. Reginald*

These are the times that try men's
souls.   *—Tom Paine*

Let other pens dwell on guilt and misery. —*Jane Austen*

Standing, as I do, in the view of God and eternity I realize that patriotism is not enough. I must have no hatred or bitterness towards anyone.

—Edith Cavell